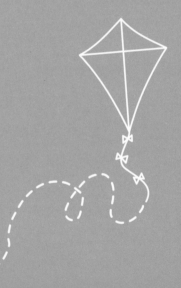

# You're It!

Published in the United Kingdom by
Collins & Brown
10 Southcombe Street
London
W14 0RA

An imprint of Anova Books Company Ltd

Distributed in the United States and Canada by Sterling Publishing Co. Inc.
387 Park Avenue South, New York, NY 10016

ISBN 978-1-84340-637-2

A CIP catalogue for this book is available from the British Library.

10 9 8 7 6 5 4 3 2 1

Reproduction by Mission Productions, Hong Kong

Printed by Everbest Printing Co Ltd, China

This book can be ordered direct from the publisher at www.anovabooks.com

# You're It!

## A Hop, Skip and Jump Through Childhood Games

### Katie Hewett

**COLLINS & BROWN**

# Contents

# Introduction

When I was young our games involved three things: imagination, inventiveness and, above all, an awful lot of energy. It seems a world away from the games of today that require a television, a console and a nimble trigger finger. *You're It!* takes us back in time to days when the summers seemed endless, jelly and ice cream were always served at parties, and you could still buy Marathons and Opal Fruits.

I have included as many games as I could remember and have tried to make the rules as accurate as possible. Some games I could remember as if I had played them yesterday, others required a little more research. There are some classic ball games, among them my absolute favourite – Rounders. There are also several wide games, the mainstay of Scout and Guide meetings and PGL holidays. I can still remember getting lost in the long grass during a game of Fox and Hounds! Now that I have my own children I'm delighted about the number of venues that can provide birthday parties, but I have also developed a whole new respect for my mother, who organised, catered for and devised entertainment for two children's parties every year for about ten years. My family holidays usually involved a beach and I have been lucky enough to live near the sea in many of my homes as I was growing up, so beach games are very close to my heart and I have included some of my favourites. At school we had to spend a great deal of time outside and the hall monitors always made sure we couldn't sneak back in. So we had to get creative – with chalk, rope, marbles, pieces of elastic or even just ourselves. At my school we elevated Hopscotch and French Skipping to an art form and we were proud of it!

Writing this book has certainly been a trip down memory lane to my childhood, but it has also encouraged me to play these games with my children. I hope they will pass them on to their friends, too. Now it's your turn – so go on, you're it!

# Wide Games

Designed to be played where there is a lot of open space, wide games represented the most fun you could have out of doors as a child – whether it was the adrenalin rush of Bulldog, the tension of Hide and Seek, or the joy of the victory shout when you got Back to Base.

# Tag

I knew this game as 'It' – isn't it funny how the best games are often the most simple?

## How to Play

Tag can be played with two or more people – but generally the more the merrier. One person is 'It' and chases and tries to catch the other players. When they catch someone that player becomes 'It', and so on. It's helpful to include a rule that if you are caught you are not allowed to immediately tag the person who caught you, to stop the game from getting repetitive.

## NAME-CALLING

You may also know this game as 'It', 'Tig', 'Tick' or 'Catch'.

## Variations
• • • • • • • • • •

• In 'Off-ground Tag' the people being chased are safe if they can find a place that is off the ground, e.g. a tree trunk, a climbing frame or a bench.
• 'Kiss Chase' is another version of this game where the boys are all 'It' and have to chase the girls until they can catch and kiss them (or vice versa).

# Tails

**Adding tails is a good way to add a bit of variety to a game of 'It'. Tails can be made from anything – ribbons, string, fabric or rope – whatever you can find.**

## How to Play

Choose one person to be 'It' and give the other players a 'tail' to tuck into the waistband of their pants/skirts. When the game starts the person who's 'It' chases the others and tries to snatch their tails. If a player's tail is caught then he or she is out of the game.

## And the Winner Is …

The last person with a tail.

## Variation
• • • • • • • • •

This can be made into a team tag game. One example is 'Cat and Mouse'. In this game a small number of catchers or 'cats' chase the rest of the players, the 'mice', and try to snatch their tails. When all the tails have been caught the cat with the highest number wins.

# Coast Guards and Smugglers

**This is a brilliant game to play in the woods or in sand dunes with lots of scrub.**

## How to Play

Divide the players into two teams: a small number of 'coast guards' (2–3) with everyone else as 'smugglers' (8 or more). The coast guards then set up a base to be the 'jail'.

The coast guards shut their eyes and count to 30 so that the smugglers can run away and hide. The coast guards then have to catch all the smugglers. Smugglers are caught when a coast guard 'tags' them, and they are then automatically sent to jail. They can only be freed from jail if they are tagged by another smuggler that is still free. If time runs out and the smugglers have not all been caught, points can be awarded for the number of smugglers in jail.

### Tip

• If there are lots of potential hiding places it may help to have a few more coast guards, so that the smugglers don't have too much of an advantage.

# Fox and Hounds

*I used to love this game – when I was running from the 'hounds' I would imagine I was an escaping prisoner or the hero in a film!*

## You Will Need

Pieces of wool, whistles.

## How to Play

For six or more players. Divide the players into groups of 'foxes' and 'hounds' (25% foxes to 75% hounds is a good ratio). Tie a piece of wool around each fox's wrist and give them a whistle. At the start of the game give the foxes a head start of up to five minutes – they can either hide or keep moving. When the time is up the hounds can start the chase. After the head start is over, the foxes must blow their whistles every 30 seconds to give the hounds a clue as to their whereabouts.

If a hiding fox is spotted by a hound, he or she must make an effort to run away and escape being caught.

## Catching the Fox

If a hound catches a fox they must remove the piece of wool from his or her wrist and they are then out. The game ends when all the foxes have been caught.

# Variations

• • • • • • • • • •

• A time limit can be set for the game and if any of the foxes are still free after the time is up then they are the winners.
• The foxes can be given a bag of flour each instead of a whistle. They then have to drop some flour at 30-second intervals to act as 'scent' for the hounds to follow.
• If you have neither flour nor whistles then the foxes can just howl at 30-second intervals!

# Back to Base

**I went to four different elementary schools and this game was popular at each of them – albeit with slightly different names. I even played it at university!**

## How to Play

For three or more players. First everyone agrees on a base – like a tree, a rock or a wall – that players can touch back to and be safe. The person who's 'It' (the finder) covers their eyes and counts to 100. He or she then goes to find the hiders.

When a hider is spotted, he or she races back to touch base before the finder while shouting 'Back to Base 1-2-3!' If the finder reaches base first, then the hider is out.

While the finder is creeping around trying to seek out all the hiding places, the hiders have to look out for an opportunity to race back to base. The first person to get back to base is 'It' for the next game.

## Watch Out For

Sneaky players hiding just round the corner or a short distance away ready to jump out and touch base the moment the finder walks away.

## NAME-CALLING

You may also know this game as: '1-2-3-in', 'Nine-nine-in', 'Kick the Can', '40-40' or 'Block Home'.

**Tip**

• **If you've got a super-slow finder, you can allow them to count people out by running and 'tagging' the hider instead of racing them back to base. This means that younger children, who wouldn't have a chance at out-sprinting older children, can be included more easily.**

## Variation
• • • • • • • • •

Caught players can be put into 'jail' – an agreed area near to the base but not blocking it. If a player gets back to base before 'It' then the caught players are freed and 'It' has to count again.

# Bulldog

*A few bumps were part and parcel of this game. I just used to shut my eyes, run for it and hope for the best!*

## How to Play

For five to 25 players. One member is the 'bulldog' in the middle of the playing area. The other players line UP in a designated 'safe' area at one end. When the bulldog shouts 'Bulldog!', all the players run from one end of the playing area to the safe area at the other end without being caught.

To catch someone, the bulldog has to hold on to a player for as long as they take to shout '1, 2, 3, bulldog!' This player then joins the bulldog in the middle and helps to catch the players on the next run. The winner is the last to be caught.

## NAME-CALLING

You may also know this game as: 'Red Rover', 'British Bulldogs', 'Cock-a-Rooster' or 'Pom-Pom-Pull-Away'.

### JOKES WE USED TO TELL
**Patient: Doctor, Doctor, I keep thinking I'm a pair of curtains.**
Doctor: Pull yourself together!

# Stuck in the Mud

*I have memories of standing and waiting desperately to be freed while playing this game – it can't have been for long but it used to seem like forever.*

## How to Play

Choose one player to be 'It'. When the game starts, he or she has to catch or tag as many people as possible. Players who are caught must stand still with their legs apart, as though they are stuck in the mud.

## Getting Unstuck

For a stuck player to be freed, a player who has not yet been caught must crawl through his or her legs.

## A Sticky End

The game ends when everyone is stuck in the mud.

**Tip**

- **For more than ten people it's probably a good idea to start with two people being 'It'.**
- **If crawling through legs is tricky, players who are stuck can stand with their arms out, so that other players can duck under their arms to free them.**

# Capture the Flag

**This used to feel like proper medieval warfare – we were brave soldiers defending our flag and our honour!**

## You Will Need
Two flags or other portable markers.

## How to Play
You will need a playing area the size of, at least, a soccer pitch and then split the players into two even teams of five or more. Each team then decides on a base or 'jail' and a place inside the game's boundary to plant their 'flag', which can be an actual flag or just a marker. The teams must show one another where their flags have been placed. The aim of the game is to capture the other team's flag.

Once the flag has been placed, the defending team has to stay at least 5m (16ft) away from it to allow the opposing team the opportunity to capture it. During the game there is a safe area of about 10m (33ft) around each base. Make sure the safe areas are clearly understood by each team to avoid disagreements!

## Taking a 'Life'
Starting from their own bases, players must try to capture the other team's flag. If they touch or tag a member of the

opposite team who is trespassing within their safe area, the trespasser loses a life and is sent to 'jail', only to be freed if they are tagged by a free member of their own team. The freed player must then go back to his or her own base to get another life before rejoining the game.

If a player captures the flag of the opposing team but is tagged on the way back to base, the flag must be left at that spot, and the defending players must stay 5m (16ft) away as before.

## The Winner

The winning team is the one who captures the other team's flag and gets it back to their base or, if time has run out, the team who has managed to catch the most members of the opposing team.

• **Teams can appoint certain members to be jailers, roaming guards or attackers.**

### JOKES WE USED TO TELL
**What do you call a deer with no eyes?**
No idea.

# Hide and Seek

**An all-time classic. Isn't it funny how loud your breathing sounds when you're hiding?**

## How to Play

Can be played with two players, but more is definitely better. One person is the seeker, while everyone else hides within a designated area. The seeker then covers his or her eyes and counts up to an agreed number to give everyone time to hide. When the seeker finishes counting they shout, 'Coming, ready or not!' When a person is found they are out immediately, they don't need to be tagged or caught. The game continues until the last person is found and this person is the winner.

## Variation
• • • • • • • • •

'Hide the Object', perhaps better known as 'Hunt the Thimble', is a game where the person who is 'It' hides an object (usually a small one, like a thimble) and the other players have to find it. The object can either be hidden or placed in plain sight. If players need a hint you can tell them whether they are 'warm' or 'cold'.

# Sardines

**This is Hide and Seek in reverse. It would often end with funny hiding positions and stifled giggles!**

## How to Play
One person hides while the rest count to a prearranged number. When the time's up the players go in search of the hider. When a player finds the hider, instead of ending the game by telling everyone else, he or she quietly squeezes into the hiding place, too.

## Last One Standing
The loser is the last one to find the hiding place – by which time the other players will be squashed together like sardines. The loser usually then has to hide first in the next round.

### JOKES WE USED TO TELL
**What does Batman's mother call when it's time to come and eat?**
Dinner dinner dinner dinner, BATMAN!

# Scavenger Hunt

This game requires plenty of resourcefulness and ingenuity – it's like being a pirate and a detective at the same time! American gossip columnist Elsa Maxwell (1883–1963), who was renowned for her high society parties, has been credited with the introduction of the scavenger hunt as a form of entertainment for her guests.

## How to Play

First the organiser prepares a list of items that the participants, either as individuals or as a team, have to find and collect – usually without paying for them, hence the term 'scavenger' – within a prearranged time limit.

The winner is the first person or team to collect all the items, or the person/team who has collected the most items when the time runs out.

## Variation
• • • • • • • •

Instead of physically collecting items, players can be asked to take photographs of the items, or of themselves at particular locations, or they could be asked to perform certain tasks (or a combination of all three!).

# **Top Ten:** Delicious School Dinners

Everyone remembers their school dinners, no matter if it was the savoury spam fritters or the sweet suet of spotted dick. Many old-school dinners sounded exotic too, which has helped us remember them — even if they didn't always taste that nice! These were my Top Ten canteen classics...

1. Iced finger buns
2. Spotted dick
3. Jam roly-poly
4. Traffic-Light Tarts
5. Semolina Pudding
6. Beef cobbler
7. Pink custard
8. Spam fritters
9. Tapioca
10. Toad in the Hole

# Ball Games

One of the essential pieces of play equipment. We weren't fussy – whether it was a grubby tennis ball, rock-hard cricket ball, saggy football or plastic beach ball, sometimes all we needed was one ball to play dozens of games.

# Catch

My sister's godfather used to spend hours throwing a tennis ball up into the air for us all to catch. And I can still do it ... well, most of the time.

## You Will Need
A ball – any size will do.

## How to Play
Catch is the name given to a game played with two or more people that involves tossing or throwing a ball of any kind back and forth between the players. There are many different versions of catch but here are just a couple.

## Down on One Knee
Two or more of you face one another, or form a circle, and throw the ball between you. If you miss the ball you must go down on one knee, but continue to throw and catch the ball. On the second miss, you go down on both knees. The third miss requires one hand be put behind your back. The fourth miss means that you are out. A successful catch at any of these stages, however, means that you can move up one position if you have previously been penalised. The last person remaining is the winner.

# 500

Good for your math as well as your catching skills, this game works your mind as well as your body.

## You Will Need

A racket – a tennis racket is best – and a ball.

## How to Play

This is a good game for larger groups and requires a bit of space. One person stands at the front with the racket and ball while everyone else spreads out. The hitter sends the ball up into the air. As the ball begins its descent he or she shouts out how many points the ball is worth for this round – somewhere between 50 and 500.

Whoever catches the ball wins that number of points. If you miss then the same number of points are deducted from your overall score (you can go into negative points!).

The first person to reach 500 points is the winner and becomes the hitter for the next round.

> ### JOKES WE USED TO TELL
> ......................................
> ### Why do cows have bells?
> Because their horns don't work!

# Rounders

**Much as I hate to blow my own trumpet I used to be a bit of a Rounders queen and a pretty useful bowler to boot. I have to admit, though, it did represent the pinnacle of my sporting career!**

## You Will Need
A bat, a ball, six markers, such as cones or stumps.

## How to Play
Divide players into two teams of about nine: this gives the fielding team a bowler, a backstop (to stop the ball when it goes behind the hitter), a fielder for each of the four bases, and three outfielders.

Arrange four of the markers in a square within the playing area, which needs to be about 17m (56ft) deep, to mark out the bases, allowing about 12m (40ft) between each base. Then place one marker between bases 1 and 4, a few paces towards the centre of the square, where the batter should stand, and another marker a few paces closer still to the centre of the square, for the bowler. Toss a coin to see which team will bat first. The winning team is the one which scores the most rounders.

## Batting

Each player on the batting team takes it in turn to hit the ball far enough so that he or she has enough time to run around the outside of all four bases before the ball is returned to the bowler. If this is achieved the player scores a 'rounder'.

If the batter doesn't have time to complete a rounder before the ball is returned from the outfield, he or she may stop at bases 1, 2 or 3; they will then run on to complete the circuit when the next or subsequent batter has started running. You can run even if you don't hit the ball – just make sure you reach first base before the backstop can throw it there!

When the ball is hit behind the batter, he or she can only run as far as first base. If you have only one bat it must be dropped (not thrown) inside the batting area for the next batter to pick up.

## Bowling

A 'good ball' is bowled underarm and must reach the batter below head level, above knee level and within reach of the outstretched rounders bat. A ball bowled outside this area is a 'no ball'. A batter can hit a no ball if he or she chooses. This can be an advantage as you cannot be caught out from a no ball. Alternatively, the batter can ignore the no ball and wait for the bowler to bowl a good ball.

## How to Be Out

A batter is out if a fielder catches the ball he or she has hit before it touches the ground, if the fielder touches the post the batter is running to with the ball before the batter reaches it, or if he or she leaves a post before the subsequent batter has started to run. He or she must remain in contact with the post at all times when not actually running and cannot return to a post already left behind. When all the players are out the teams swap places.

## Variation
• • • • • • • • •

Some games might include the opportunity to score a 'half rounder' by getting all the way round but stopping at one or more bases.

# Football Rounders

Who needs a bat? Here are some ways to enjoy the
excitement of Rounders even if you don't have the keys
to the sports cupboard.

## You Will Need
Football or similar-sized ball, six markers.

## How to Play
The rules of this game are the same as for Rounders, but the
bowler rolls the ball underarm along the ground and the
'batter' kicks the ball instead of trying to hit it with a bat.

## Variations
• • • • • • • • • •

• Throwing Rounders is played without a bowler or
a backstop. The 'batter' or 'thrower' stands on the
batting spot and throws the ball as far as they can, then
tries to run around as many bases as possible before
being run out.
• In Danish Rounders the 'batter' hits the ball with his
or her hand. They can't stop at bases and must try and
score a rounder on each throw.

# French Cricket

Traditionally this was very much a game played by 'gentlemen' – hence the use of the term 'he' to refer to the players here. It can get very competitive so sitting on the sidelines enjoying the sunshine was often thought to be a much better option!

## You Will Need

A cricket bat or tennis racket, a ball.

## How to Play

This is a game for three or more players. The playing area is a circle that you can mark out with the bat. The size of the circle can vary according to the number/ability of players, but a rough guide is that the bowler stands about six good paces from the batsman, and the fielders make a circle around them.

## Batting

The batsman stands in the centre of the circle and marks out his 'crease', using the tip of his bat to draw a circle at arm's length. The crucial rule in French Cricket is that the batsman's feet must not move during play. He can play shots behind him by holding his bat in either hand and twisting his body around, but his feet must stay still. A run is scored each time the ball is hit successfully outside the crease. A ball hit over the boundary of the playing circle scores six runs, and a ball that reaches the boundary but bounces first scores four runs.

## Bowling

For the first ball thrown the bowler must stand about 5.5m (18ft) from the batsman. Balls must be bowled underarm. After the initial throw the ball is bowled from wherever it is picked up and that person then becomes the bowler. If the ball reaches the boundary then it is returned to the original position.

## How to Be Out

The batsman is out if he:

- **is hit on the legs by the ball (bowled out).**
- **moves his feet at any time, or touches the ground with his hand, even if his feet remain stationary.**
- **hits a ball that is brought to rest by a fielder before the ball has hit the ground (caught out).**
- **does not hit the ball out of the crease circle.**
- **hits the ball twice before it touches a fielder.**

# Four Square

Like many apparently simple games, some players have elevated Four Square to an art form. These are just the basics.

## You Will Need

Chalk to mark out the playing area, a large ball such as a football or volleyball, an asphalt area like a playground.

## How to Play

This is a game for four players at a time, although other players can wait on the sidelines to be swapped in. Draw a square 2.5m x 2.5m (8ft x 8ft), and divide it into four equal squares. The top left square is number 1, top right is number 2, bottom right is number 3, and bottom left is number 4.

The object of the game is to gain the number 1 square and defend the position against the three attackers. The number 1 square is sometimes called the 'King' while the others (in descending order of importance) are the 'Queen' (2), 'Prince' (3) and 'Princess' (4). Each of the four players guards his/her own square. Decide between you who gets to start in each square, or you can draw lots. The number 1 player or King serves the ball by bouncing it in his or her square once and then hitting it with an open hand towards one of the other squares. The receiving player allows the ball to bounce in his or her square and then hits the ball to any other player. Play continues until one of the following things occur:

- **A player hits the ball (or is hit by the ball) before it bounces once in their square.**
- **A player does not hit the ball before it bounces twice.**
- **A player hits the ball and it bounces outside of the playing area.**

When one of these situations occurs the player concerned moves to the lowest ranking square and the other players then move up to higher ranking squares to fill the vacancies. If there are more players than squares, the player must leave the game and go to the back of the line, and the person at the front of the line moves onto the lowest square and starts to play.

## JOKES WE USED TO TELL

**How did the dinner lady get an electric shock?**
She stepped on a bun and a currant went up her leg!

# Wall Ball

**Throwing a ball against the wall is fine when you're by yourself – but is so much better when there are friends around.**

## You Will Need
A tennis ball or other bouncy ball; a large, flat wall.

## How to Play
This game works best with two to four players. If your group is larger then the remaining players can wait in a line until someone is out and then the first person can take over.

First, one of the four players throws the ball directly against the wall, the ball is allowed to bounce once after it has hit the wall, and then one of the four players (including the one who threw it) tries to catch it.

If a player throws the ball and it bounces before it reaches the wall, or if a player fumbles or drops the ball during play, that player has to try to run to the wall and touch it before one of the other players is able to hit the wall with the ball.

If the player reaches the wall in time play continues, but if the player is unsuccessful then this counts as a strike.

## How to Be Out
Three strikes and you're out.

# Bench Ball

**Make sure your gym shoes have plenty of grip for this one – especially if you're the one on the bench!**

## You Will Need

Two benches and a large ball like a netball.

## How to Play

Put a bench along each end of the playing area – usually the size of a badminton court (13.4m x 6.1m/44ft x 20ft). Divide the players into two teams of 6–12, with one team on each side of the court (if you do not have a centre line then you can use cones or markers instead). Each team chooses a goalkeeper who stands on one of the two benches.

The teams score goals by passing the ball to their own goalkeeper, while he or she is standing on the bench, without it being caught by the other team. To start the umpire throws up the ball between two opposing players. The players then pass the ball between themselves until someone shoots. A goal is only valid if the goalkeeper catches the ball while standing firmly on the bench – not while falling off!

When a goal is scored the opposition restarts by throwing the ball in from the goal line (behind the bench where the goal was scored). Once a goal has been scored a different player must become the goalkeeper.

# Dodge Ball

**We played this a lot in gym lessons on wet days – I used to pull my socks up high to try and avoid bruises!**

## You Will Need

A large ball like a football – but not too hard!

## How to Play

Best for ten or more players. Choose two or more players, depending on how many there are in total, to be 'taggers'; the rest spread out within the playing area. The object is to tag the other players by hitting them with the ball below the knee. Only the taggers can pick up the ball. When players are tagged they are out and have to sit to one side. The last person remaining is the winner.

## NAME-CALLING

You may also know this game as: 'Knee Ball', 'Ball Tag'.

### JOKES WE USED TO TELL
......................................
**What goes up when the rain comes down?**
An umbrella.

# Variations

• In some versions the taggers can run with the ball, while in others they must stand still while they are holding the ball.

• Instead of sitting out when caught, players become taggers instead.

• This can be played as a team game with one team forming a circle of taggers while the other team moves about inside it. When a player is caught he or she can either sit out or join the opposing team and try and tag the people still inside the circle.

# Horse Basketball

This game requires quite a lot of skill – I was never very good at it and would have to be awarded a lot of bonus shots to have any chance of staying in!

## You Will Need

A basketball and a hoop.

## How to Play

This is a game for two or more players. For two players toss a coin to decide who's going to go first; with more players you will need to decide on an order of play.

The first player takes a shot at the hoop from anywhere they choose on the court. If they make the shot then the second player has to make the same shot from the same position on the court.

If both players manage it the play passes to the next player (or back to the first player if there's only two) who selects a new shot for the next round.

If a player misses a shot, they are assigned the first letter of the word 'horse', i.e. 'H', and the other player selects the shot in the next round. As play continues each missed shot collects the next letter in the word horse. Once a player has collected all the letters then he or she is out of the game.

Play continues until only one player is left and they are the winner.

## Remember:
• It helps if the players are well matched in terms of ability. If not then some less able players might be allowed a certain number of bonus shots so they get another chance if they miss a shot.
• By the same token certain difficult shots, the dunk for example, may not be allowed if not all the players can make that shot.

## Variations
• • • • • • • • • •

• The word 'pig' can be used instead of 'horse' for a shorter game, or 'donkey' for a longer game.
• Once a shot has been made in one place or style it cannot be repeated.
• After someone collects all the letters and is out, the person who made the last successful shot must take it again to prove it was skill and not luck. If they miss, the person who was out can have one more chance.

# **Top Ten:** Excuses For Not Doing Homework

*We've all forgotten to do homework before. The question is, did you own up...or did you tell a little lie?*

1. The dog ate it.
2. I couldn't find the answers anywhere.
3. The house was cold so we had to set fire to it to keep warm.
4. Homework?  I thought you were joking.
5. I was abducted by aliens and they only brought me back this morning.
6. It was in my backpack this morning, someone must have stolen it.
7. It fell out of my bag as I helped an old lady across the road.
8. My dad accidentally put it in his briefcase.
9. I had better things to do.
10. I didn't want to make the rest of the class look bad by doing so well.

# Party Games

Parties used to be the highlight of our week, and there was a huge amount of excitement about wearing our best clothes, eating unlimited jelly, ice cream, crisps and cake, and doing an awful lot of running about. Is it any wonder we always felt sick by the end?

# Hide the Candy

This is great for parties or even rainy days. I used to love this game because it was exciting, frustrating and rewarding all at the same time!

## You Will Need
Candy, coins, buttons or other small objects.

## How to Play
First decide on a playing area indoors – it can be one room or a number of rooms – and then choose one person to be 'It'. The other players leave the playing area for a while and he or she hides the object(s).

When the object(s) have been hidden, the players come back in and start to hunt for them. If the players need a hint the person who is 'It' can say who is 'warm' (i.e. closer to the object) or 'cold' (further away).

## Tip

• Players should look up high and down low as well as straight ahead, and if they are 'warm', make small movements until they are 'hot'. If they rush to make larger movements they may well find they get 'colder' again.

# Blind Man's Buff

**This game was great fun but when I was blindfolded I would always worry that my friends were going to trick me by leaving the room without me realising!**

## You Will Need
A blindfold.

## How to Play
One person is chosen to be 'It' and is blindfolded. He or she then walks around the room trying to tag the other players while they dodge around trying to avoid being caught. The person who is tagged is either out or becomes 'It' for the next round. Alternatively the game can continue until there's only one player left and he or she is the winner.

## Variation
• • • • • • • • •

After tagging someone, 'It' can feel their face and attempt to identify him or her; only if the tagged person is correctly identified does he or she become 'It'.

# Musical Chairs

**Fast, furious and competitive. My trick was to try and watch whoever was operating the music to see when they were going to hit the pause button.**

## You Will Need

Chairs – one fewer than there are people – and a music player.

## How to Play

Arrange the chairs back to back in a line. All the players stand in a circle around the chairs. Agree in advance which direction to go, and then when the music starts walk, march or dance around the chairs. As soon as the music stops each player needs to find an empty chair and sit down as quickly as possible. The player left without a chair is out.

For the next round take one chair away and do the same again. Continue until there is just one chair and two players. When the music stops the first player to sit down is the winner.

---

### JOKES WE USED TO TELL
................................................

**What happened to the wooden car with wooden wheels and a wooden engine?**
It wooden go.

---

# Variation

'Islands' is a similar game that uses newspaper instead of chairs. Spread out sheets of newspaper (one for every five players) and scatter them around the floor of the room. When the music stops, everyone has to squish together and stand on a piece of newspaper. Anyone not standing on newspaper after a few seconds (or failing that, the last person to get on the newspaper) is out. Every few rounds remove a sheet of newspaper, and when there's only one sheet left fold it in half until only one person is left – the winner.

# Musical Statues

**Standing still should have been an easy thing to achieve, so why did we always used to find it so hard? Maybe all that sugar had something to do with it …!**

## You Will Need
A music player.

## How to Play
When the music starts the players dance around the room. When it stops they must immediately 'freeze' while the judge (usually a grown-up) has a good look around to see who is wobbling. Anyone caught moving before the music starts again is out. The game keeps going until only one person is left, and they are the winner.

## Variation
· · · · · · · · ·

In 'Musical Bumps' the players have to sit down on the floor when the music stops. The last person to sit down in each round is out and the last one left in is the winner. Be careful not to land too hard!

# Balloon Race

**This game was guaranteed to produce three things: lots of noise, burst balloons and red faces.**

## You Will Need

Lots of balloons – one for each team and plenty of spares!

## How to Play

A game for two (or more) teams of four-plus people. Each team forms a line, the first player holds the balloon between their knees and passes it to the next player in the line without using their hands. When the balloon gets to the end of the line that player runs (as best they can!) to the front of the line with the balloon still between their knees and the process starts again. Play continues until the person who started returns to the front of the line and the team then sit down. The first team to sit down is the winner.

## Variation

• • • • • • • • •

Instead of using their knees the first player passes the balloon backwards over his or her head; the next player then passes it between his or her legs to the person behind, who passes it over his or her head, and so on.

# Pin the Tail on the Donkey

*I loved the moment when I got to take off my blindfold and see where I had put the tail – I'm not sure I ever managed to get it in the right place!*

## You Will Need

A large picture of a donkey (or other animal with a tail); tails (pieces of rope or wool will do), sticky tape, a pin or adhesive putty at one end; a blindfold or scarf; a pencil to write each player's name next to their tail when they have placed it.

## How to Play

Blindfold the first player and turn them around three times, then give them the tail, making it clear which is the sticky end. Guide them towards the picture so they can try and stick on the tail. The player who gets closest is the winner.

### Tip

- Touching the donkey where the tail needs to be placed before your turn will help you remember how high you will have to raise your arm.

# The Farmer's in His Den

**Circle games like this are always fun for young children.**

## How to Play

Choose one player to be the Farmer while the rest form a circle around him or her. The players in the circle hold hands and walk around the Farmer singing:

**The farmer's in his den, the farmer's in his den,
E-i-adio, the farmer's in his den.
The farmer wants a wife, the farmer wants a wife,
E-i-adio, the farmer wants a wife.**

The farmer chooses one of the other players to join him inside the circle as his 'wife'. The song starts again, but with the words, 'The wife wants a child ...' and another player is chosen to go inside the circle as the 'child'. The song continues with 'The child wants a dog ...' and then 'The dog wants a bone ...' (and any others you can remember!) with a new player being chosen to join the farmer each time. The game ends with 'We all pat the dog ...' and the players all pat the head of the player that has been chosen to be the dog.

# Untying the Knot

This team game requires co-operation, logical thinking and a bit of flexibility. Go on, have a go!

## How to Play

This can be played in one or more groups depending on the number of players. In each group there should be an even number of players (between six and ten works well). The players stand in a tight circle, hold their left hand out to the right side of their bodies and take hold of someone else's right hand. Then they do the same with their right hand to their left hand side. They have now formed a human knot, with everyone's arms crossed across the front of their bodies.

The object of this game is for the players to untangle the knot without letting go of each other's hands. They will have to turn around and weave under and over each other's arms but it is possible!

When more than one team is playing, the winner is the first team to sit down having successfully freed themselves.

## Tip

• Get players to link up their hands easily by referring to how they would during 'Auld Lang Syne' on New Year's Eve!

# Pass the Orange

**This game was good if you were passing the orange to someone you liked or even had a crush on.**

## You Will Need
An orange, or similar-sized fruit (one for each team).

## How to Play
Each team stands in a line. The first player in each team tucks the orange under his or her chin and passes it to the next player with no hands. When the orange reaches the end of the line the last player runs to the front of the line and the process begins again. Play continues until the first person returns to the front of the line and the team then sit down. The first team to sit down is the winner.

# Variation
• • • • • • • • • •

Another favourite uses a spoon tied to a long piece of string (long enough to join all the team members together). The first person threads the spoon down their sweater and the next person has to thread it up theirs and so on until all the team members are 'sewn' together. The first team to get the spoon to the end of the line wins.

# Simon Says

**Dating back hundreds of years, this game has been played in a variety of forms all over the world, in countries as diverse as Brazil, Finland, China and India.**

## How to Play

Choose one player to be Simon while the rest of the players line up about 4m (12ft) away. Simon then gives commands to the players, such as, 'Simon says, put your hands on your head'. He or she then checks to make sure everyone has followed the instruction correctly. Then Simon might say, 'Simon says, stand on one leg'. If Simon gives an instruction without first saying 'Simon says' then all those who follow it are out of the game. The winner is the last player remaining.

## How to Catch People Out

• Give the orders quickly, one after the other.

• Cut the orders short, saying 'Simon says do this', and get the players to copy your action. Do this a number of times and then say 'Do this' – and quite a few people will usually follow your lead.

• Make it appear as if you are not playing the game for a moment and say something like, 'Can you come a bit closer?'. Sneaky, I know …

# Oranges and Lemons

This traditional game is based on the old English rhyme referring to the bells of several churches around the City of London.

## How to Play

Facing each other, two players hold each other's hands and lift them up to form an arch. The other players form pairs, line up and walk through the arch while singing this song:

Oranges and lemons
Say the bells of St Clements.
You owe me five farthings
Say the bells of St Martins.
When will you pay me?
Say the bells of Old Bailey.
When I grow rich
Say the bells of Shoreditch.
When will that be?
Say the bells of Stepney.
I do not know
Says the great bell at Bow.

**Here comes a candle to light you to bed**
**Here comes a chopper to chop off your head**
**Chop, chop, chop, chop**
**The last man's head!**

The pairs keep filing through the arch until the song reaches the last two lines. At this point the players making the arch start making a chopping action with their arms, and on the last word – 'head!' – they catch the pair who happen to be passing through. This pair then forms another arch alongside the original pair, making it harder for the remaining players to escape the next round, and so on. The last pair left are the winners.

# Variation
• • • • • • • • •

Instead of forming another arch when they are caught, the two children 'chopped' each round can line up one behind each of the original pair. When all the children have been caught the two teams can have a 'tug of war' to see which one is stronger.

# Pass the Parcel

Now I have my own children I've discovered just how long it takes to wrap the parcel for this game – I have now thanked my mother all over again for the many parcels she prepared for my parties over the years.

## You Will Need
A prize wrapped in one more layer of wrapping paper or newspaper than there are players, and a music player.

## How to Play
All the players sit on the floor in a circle. When the music starts the parcel is continuously passed around. Holding on to the parcel while the music is still playing is strictly forbidden!

When the music stops, the person holding on to the parcel removes one layer of paper. The music starts again and the parcel is passed around until the next time the music stops. When the parcel is down to its final layer the person holding the parcel when the music stops this time wins the prize.

### JOKES WE USED TO TELL
**How does an elephant hide in a cherry tree?**
He paints his toenails red.

# The Chocolate Game

**I was always desperate to do well in this game, but with so many goodies to look forward to at teatime, this now seems rather surprising.**

## You Will Need

A big bar of chocolate; a knife and fork; a hat; a scarf; a pair of gloves; a die.

## How to Play

All the players sit in a circle with the chocolate, knife and fork, and clothes in the middle. One player starts by rolling the die, which is then passed to the next person in the circle to throw, until someone throws a six. This person then has to put on the hat, scarf and gloves as quickly as he or she can and then, using the knife and fork, tries to eat as much of the chocolate as possible before the next person throws a six.

The game continues until all of the chocolate has been eaten – or until the players start to feel ill!

# Dressing-up Race

**This is basically a relay race with a difference – the difference is that this is a lot funnier.**

## You Will Need

For each team you will need an assortment of clothes (hats, scarves, gloves, raincoat, boots) and three markers (cones are good).

## How to Play

Divide the players into teams of three or more. For each of the teams place one of the markers on the starting line, another one 3m (10ft) away on a mid-line with the pile of clothes, and a third 3m (10ft) further away on an end line that the players have to touch before returning to the mid-line and taking off the clothes.

When someone says 'go', the first player in each team runs to the mid-line and puts on all of the clothes. He or she then run to the end line or around the marker, then runs back to the mid-line, takes off the clothes, and then races back to the start line to tag the next person in the team who then does the same. They keep going until all the players have completed the race.

The winner is the first team to finish.

# Steal the Bacon

Historically bacon was regarded as a valuable commodity, hence the phrase 'bringing home the bacon' when referring to a family's breadwinner! Perhaps this game derived from a less honest way of earning a living!

## You Will Need
A bean bag, hat, scarf or other item to be the 'bacon'.

## How to Play
You will need a leader and two equal teams of five or more players, who must stand in two lines facing one another, about 4.5m (15ft) apart. Place the 'bacon' in the middle.

The players of both teams are each given a number, starting with one (so that each number has two corresponding players, one in each team). When the leader calls out a number the two players try to run into the middle and snatch the bacon and get back to their line without being tagged by the opposite number. A successful bacon run wins a point for their team. If he or she is tagged then no one gets a point.

For a more challenging version of the game, the leader can call out a simple maths problem instead of just a number: for example, 'two times two', or 'five minus two'.

The team with the most points at the end of the game wins.

# Kim's Game

**This game first appeared in a book by Rudyard Kipling and is named after the book's hero. It has since been adopted by the Scouting movement and by the military to help develop observational skills.**

## You Will Need

A tray of about 12 household items (such as a cup, saucer, ball of string, pen etc.); a cloth to cover it; pieces of paper and pens (one for each player).

## How to Play

Put the tray where all the players can see it. Uncover the items and let the players memorise them for a minute. Cover the tray again with the cloth and then ask the players to write down as many items as they can remember for another minute. The winner is the player who remembers the most items.

## Variation
• • • • • • • • •

For younger children you can show the players the tray, ask them to close their eyes and then take one of the items away. When they open their eyes, the first one to shout out the name of the missing item wins that round.

# Balloon Stomp

**Not a game for those wearing dainty party shoes – sneakers or even Dr Marten boots are a better idea!**

## You Will Need

Balloons (at least two per player), if you have teams then each team needs a different colour; ribbons or string to tie to the balloons; a music player; a balloon pump.

## How to Play

Tie a balloon around each player's ankles. Players can play as individuals or as teams of three or more.

When the music starts the players move around the room trying not to burst their balloons. As soon as the music stops they try to burst the balloons belonging to members of the opposing team(s), while protecting their own balloons. When the music starts again the stomping has to stop!

When both your balloons have been popped you are out. At the end, the team (or person) with the most balloons intact wins.

---

### JOKES WE USED TO TELL
..........................................
**Doctor, doctor, I can't get to sleep.**
Lie on the edge of the bed and you'll soon drop off!

---

# Doughnut Game

Another opportunity to eat sugary food, this game always got us very excited. The version played with apples is still fun but doughnuts definitely used to have the edge!

## You Will Need
A length of washing line; ring doughnuts (one for each player); 25cm (12in) pieces of string (one for each doughnut).

## How to Play
A game for four or more players. Can be a team game if you have more people. String the doughnuts along the washing line at regular intervals. When the game starts the players have to eat a doughnut without using their hands, dropping it, or licking their lips (however tempting it may be...!). The first person to eat their whole doughnut wins.

This can also be played with apples, which are a lot healthier, it's but much more difficult!

Apple bobbing, often associated with Halloween, is a twist on this game. Apples are placed in a washing-up bowl full of water and the players take it in turns to splash around and try to pick an apple out of the water with their teeth.

# I Went to the Shops ...

This is a classic memory game that used to be popular in schools as well as at parties. Well, they do say learning should be fun ...

## How to Play

Everyone sits in a circle. Someone begins by saying, 'I went to the shops and bought ...' and chooses something beginning with the letter 'A', for example 'an apple'. The next person then says, 'I went to the shops and bought an apple ...' and then adds an item beginning with the letter 'B' and so on.

If you forget the order or get any item wrong then you're out. The last person left is the winner.

### Tip

• This game can get confusing, especially when people drop out. It often helps to look at each person while you're reciting the list, to help you remember what they said.

# Treasure Hunt

**This game was fun anyway, but the promise of a prize at the end made it even more exciting.**

## You Will Need

A selection of candy and prizes, or slips of paper containing clues that finally lead to the main prize or 'treasure'.

## How to Play

The simplest treasure hunts can just involve looking for candy hidden around the house or garden. Whoever finds a candy gets to keep (or eat!) it.

More sophisticated hunts begin with a clue that leads to a location where there will be another clue, and so on. The clues might be straightforward ('The next clue is behind the chair') or more cryptic ('The next clue is behind something blue').

Or a treasure hunter might be given a map showing the location of the treasure and heads off, either alone or in a team, to try and find it.

### JOKES WE USED TO TELL
...................................................
**Why did the germ cross the microscope?**
To get to the other slide.

# Squeak Piggy Squeak

**A good way to find out how well you know your friends.**

## How to Play

For six or more players. Choose one player to be the 'farmer' while the others are the 'piggies'. The piggies form a circle and the farmer sits in the middle, wearing a blindfold.

Spin the farmer round three times and then he must walk (or stumble!) over to the circle of piggies, and sit on one of their laps, saying, 'Squeak Piggy Squeak!' The chosen piggy does his or her best squeak and the farmer has to guess the name of the squeaker. If the farmer guesses correctly, the piggy becomes the farmer in the next round. If the farmer gets it wrong then he or she stays for the next round.

## Variation
• • • • • • • • •

Instead of squeaking the piggy can 'oink' or grunt like a pig. If the farmer guesses right, the piggy is out and the farmer takes his or her place. The piggy that is out then chooses another player to be the farmer.

# Tin Can Alley

**Just like a sideshow at the fairground, this game was a really fun way to develop your target skills.**

## You Will Need

Ten empty cans and some bean bags.

## How to Play

For three or more players. Stack the cans in a pyramid on a table with four on the bottom, then three, then two, then one.

Each player is given three bean bags and must try and knock down all the cans – make sure the players are standing well enough back to make the game a challenge. If none of the players are able to knock down all the cans then the one that manages to knock down the most in each round is the winner.

## Variations
• • • • • • • • • •

• As the game continues you can move the start line further and further back each time to make the game harder.
• You could also build the cans up again after each throw and add up the points scored each time.

# **Top Ten:** Classic Car Games

Whether it was a long weekend excursion down to the coast or popping round to Grandma's on a rainy afternoon, driving the family had the potential to become a stressful affair. To keep the peace, many families made up their own car games to keep the children entertained – but there are also the classics that everyone will remember...

1. I Spy!
2. Silent Counting
3. What Am I?
4. Rock, Paper, Scissors
5. Pub Cricket
6. Treasure Hunt
7. Backseat Hide and Seek
8. What Am I Counting?
9. The Never-ending Sentence
10. Backwards Spelling

# Beach Games

I always feel a real sense of freedom
when I first arrive at the beach —
the wide expanse of sand, shingle
or pebbles, the sea stretching off
into the distance, and the arch of
the sky overhead. That first breath
with its salty tang is exhilarating
and opportunities for having fun
are endless.

# Sandcastles

As a child the best thing in the world is knocking over a single sandcastle someone has built for you. And as you get older building them yourself is just as satisfying. Believe me, it has been elevated to an art form.

## You Will Need

Spades, buckets, moulds, trowel. Plastic knives and lolly sticks are also useful for shaping smaller features.

## How to Build a Sandcastle

If you want your sandcastle to last, its location is quite important — it needs to be near enough to the water's edge that the sand is damp enough to work with, but not so near that the waves come in and wash it away. Don't forget the drawbridge and the moat.

Here are some basic elements to create a majestic sandcastle:

* **Towers:** build up the height of your towers using thick circular 'slices' of damp sand until you have the height you need.
* **Walls:** press handfuls of wet sand together in a line and then build them up layer by layer. The base needs to be wider

then the rest of the wall to provide the proper support.

* **Arches:** these start off as walls and when they are ready use a small tool to start tunnelling through at the base, gradually making the hole bigger.

## Tip

- If you want to be really sophisticated a spray bottle filled with water is useful to stop the sand from drying out.
- If using a bucket, when you are filling it up give it a shake every now and then to make sure there are no gaps, and then pack the sand down firmly.
- If your bucket gets too wet and it becomes too difficult to get your sandcastles out, use fine, dry, warm sand to help it dry out.

### JOKES WE USED TO TELL
**What did the ocean say to the shore?**
Nothing, it just waved.

# Sand Art

**Sculptures and pictures are also fun to make at the beach. You may not be able to take them home but you can always take a photo.**

## Sand Sculptures

For these you need much the same equipment as for sandcastles. Choose a site with less foot traffic so your hard work doesn't get trampled. On my last holiday I saw an octopus and a frog sculpture – they looked amazing!

Use wet sand to create 'drip' sculptures with weird and wonderful shapes, or use drips to embellish your finished sculpture. Carve your sand sculpture from the top down and remember you can't go back up and do more work later – the sand will just fall down and ruin the work you have done further down.

I used to like making sand 'cakes' when I was young. I would make a ball out of damp sand and dust it with fine sand 'sugar'.

## Sand Pictures

You can use the sand itself to make your picture, but you can also use all the things you find on the beach – pebbles, shells, feathers, seaweed, grasses. Hunting for all your materials is part of the fun.

# Beach Olympics

This was always great fun but now I see that my parents had an ulterior motive – large amounts of physical activity for the children, while they sat around with drinks and stopwatches.

## You Will Need
General beach stuff like buckets and spades, some belts or scarves for three-legged races, rope for tug of war, and a watch for timed events.

## How to Play
First decide on your events. Here are some we tried:
• **Three-legged race: decide on the start and finish line, and the first team to get there wins.**
• **Long jump: draw a line in the sand. All the players run to the line and jump. Whoever jumps the furthest is the winner.**
• **Hurdles: create some hurdles using spades, cool boxes, beach bags etc. Take it in turns to run the course, and the person with the fastest time wins.**
• **Tug of war: an old favourite. Playing on sand can be tricky – it's difficult to get a grip, but dig your feet down well and you should find it easier.**

# Beach Cricket

This has developed into a professional game with its own rules and regulations, but in my day it was a lot more relaxed.

## You Will Need

A tennis ball, a bat and some stumps. You can get beach sets that include plastic stumps but we just used to use sticks, our cool box or whatever was handy. You will also need an area of beach about 50m x 50m (164ft x 164ft).

## How to Play

There is no limit to the number of players and there are no teams. Choose one person to bat and the rest of the players act as fielders. Mark out your wicket with a set of stumps at one end and a marker that the batter has to run to and from to make a run (16m/52ft). Traditionally no score is kept and the person who got the batter out becomes the next batter.

---

### JOKES WE USED TO TELL
......................................
**What is the best way to communicate with a fish?**
Drop it a line!

---

## How to Be Out

· When the ball hits the stumps, either when the ball is bowled or if the batter is 'stumped' on the way back from making a run.
· When a fielder catches the ball.

# Variations

• • • • • • • • • •

There are no hard and fast rules in beach cricket but here are some that might be useful:

• 'Tip and run': the batter has to run every time they hit the ball no matter how far it has travelled.
• 'Six and out': there may be natural boundaries that the fielders may not want to negotiate, such as more than waist-deep in the water, in the sand dunes, behind the rocks. So you can decide that if the batter hits the ball to any of these then he or she scores six runs but is automatically out.
• 'First ball' rule: you cannot be out on the first ball you face.
• 'One-hand, one-bounce': the batter can be out when they hit the ball and it bounces once provided you catch it with one hand.

# Building a Car

I was always jealous of the children whose dads had built them excellent vehicles on the beach. My dad wasn't bad but I'm not sure any of the Formula One teams would have given him a design job.

## You Will Need

Spades, hands and any other embellishments you might need for trim, aerials, hubcaps etc.

## How to Build a Car

Start with a big mound of sand and pack it down firmly. Start creating your shape remembering to carve from the top down.

First shape the bonnet and trunk, then add the tyres. Dig out your seats – do you want a sporty two-seater or a four-door family car? Then add a dashboard.

Once you have created the basic shape then you can add the final touches, such as bumpers, aerials, controls, steering wheel – anything you like.

Another favourite is to build a speedboat by digging down in the sand. Mark out your area and dig out foot wells for driver and passengers. You might want to build up the bow and the stern to give it some shape, and then sit back and relax!

# Bucket Relay Race

**A game of persistence, concentration and teamwork.**

### You Will Need
One bucket for each team.

### How to Play
Divide the players into two teams of three or more and line them up next to the shore. Put the buckets about 3m (10ft) from the water's edge.

The object of the game is for each team to fill their bucket using just their hands to hold the water. When the race starts the first member of each team scoops up a handful of water, runs to the bucket and drops the water in. They then run back to their team and the next player can go. The players keep going until the bucket is full, and the first team to fill their bucket is the winner.

## Variation
• • • • • • • • •

Use a full bucket of water and have the teams run to a marker and back before handing the bucket to the next member of the team. At the end of the race the team that has spilled the least amount of water is the winner.

# Water Balloon Toss

**This is a great way to keep cool on a hot day.**

## You Will Need
Lots of water balloons, an even number of players (four or more).

## How to Play
Divide the players into teams of two and give each pair a balloon. Get them to stand about 1m (3ft) apart. When the game starts the teams have to throw the balloons to each other, and with each successful catch the players have to take two steps back, making the distance between the players wider. The players must continue to move further and further apart with each throw.

## How to Be Out
If the balloon bursts during play then the team is disqualified.

## And the Winner Is ...
The last team with their balloon still intact.

# Limbo

**There's something about beaches that makes us want to limbo dance — at least you have a soft landing!**

## You Will Need

A long stick, a length of ribbon or a skipping rope — basically anything that can be used as the limbo pole.

## How to Play

A bit like the high jump in reverse. Two people need to hold the limbo pole or pull the rope taught.

Stand with your feet shoulder-width apart and your arms out. Using small, controlled movements, jump forwards towards the pole but don't start to bend until you reach it. Then bend your legs and lean backwards gradually as you move forwards under the pole. Wait until your head has passed under the pole and then gradually start to come up.

After each round the pole gets lower and lower. If you touch the pole or fall, you are out. The last one left in is the winner.

## Tip

- Keep your legs wide to give you a strong base.
- Make sure your head is well clear of the pole before you come up.

# Rock Pooling

**A glorious pastime. I was lucky enough to spend childhood holidays on the unspoiled coast of south-west Ireland – a rock pooler's paradise.**

## You Will Need
Shoes or boots, preferably waterproof, with a good grip: rocks can be slippery and shells can be sharp so you must protect your feet.

## How to Go Rock Pooling
Go down to the beach at low tide, find some rocks and start looking around. Watch out for the tide coming back in, as you don't want to get stuck with no way back to dry land; check the tide times when you arrive.

## What to Look For
Here are some of the things you might find when rock pooling.

**Limpets:** You will find these round, ridged shells clinging to rocks. In fact they move around the rocks very slowly, eating the weeds that they pass over.

**Barnacles:** These tiny, white crustaceans cover the rocks in their thousands. At low tide they just look like shells, but under water a little 'fan' emerges to collect plankton.

**Crabs:** These tend to live under stones and in crevices.

**Anemones:** At low tide these look like little blobs of jelly, but when the tide starts to come in their tentacles emerge in search of small prey like shrimps.

**Prawns and shrimps:** Can be hard to spot as they are quick to sense and hide from curious onlookers.

**Starfish:** A less common find but an exciting one.

**Seaweeds:** You may see many different varieties, so count how many you can find.

**Fish:** Can become stranded in rock pools, and young fish sometimes stay there until they mature.

## Remember:

• **Watch carefully and quietly – many seashore creatures are hard to spot and they will hide themselves if they think you are a threat.**

• **You will find things on top of rocks, in cracks and crevices, under stones, on seaweeds and in rock pools. If you lift a stone to see what is underneath, make sure you put it back down.**

• **Every tiny detail of a rock pool is very important to the survival of one creature or another. Therefore, leave everything just as you found it and the rock pool creatures will be there for next time.**

# Beach Bowling

A seaside version of ten-pin bowling, and just as competitive.

## You Will Need
A ball, a cup or small bucket.

## How to Play
For two or more players. First build your pins by making sandcastles with your bucket or filling the cup with sand. The classic triangle shape has four pins in the back row, three in the second row in, two in the third and one at the front.

Draw a line in the sand a short distance from the pins. From here each player take it in turns to knock down as many pins as they can — you can allow one or two throws per turn. After each turn the pins will need to be rebuilt before the next person can go. At the end of the game the person who has knocked down the most pins is the winner.

## Variation
● ● ● ● ● ● ● ● ●

Instead of building pins you can dig holes that are allocated different numbers of points. For each turn roll the ball to see how many points you can score.

# Kite Flying

**I was lucky enough to once live near a beach – it was the perfect place to fly a kite.**

## You Will Need
A kite and some wind.

## How to Fly a Kite
Single-line kites are the ones most people start with. To launch one you really need a friend to help.

In light winds, first let out about 15m (50ft) of line and get your friend to hold the kite downwind. When you are ready tell your friend to release the kite into the air. To help the kite gain height walk backwards slowly or raise your arm above your head.

In medium to strong winds, stand with your back to the wind and release the kite and line gradually.

## Remember:
• **Do not fly a kite near trees or power lines, and in rain or thunderstorms.**

# Beachcombing

Beachcombing involves searching for and finding a wide variety of curiosities that have been washed up along the shoreline by the tide. My grandmother kept a tray of finds on her windowsill and I spent many hours examining each one and imagining about where they may have come from.

## You Will Need
The same sort of footwear as for rock pooling, a bag for carrying your finds (and an extra bag for any rubbish you might find – the more you can do to preserve the environment the better), and a camera.

## How to Go Beachcombing
While it is fun to go beachcombing at any time, the best times to find interesting or unusual items are in the following conditions: the winter, early in the morning, at low tide, after a storm.

## What to Look For
Seashells, pieces of pottery, fossils, animal bones, old fishing floats, nets, stones, driftwood, sea urchins, starfish skeletons, sea glass (glass that has been worn smooth around the edges by the sea – my family calls this 'lucky glass').

# Building a Dam to the Sea

**What's better than a beach? A beach with a stream running to the sea.**

## You Will Need

Stones, wood, leaves, shells – any natural building materials you can find.

## How to Build a Dam

Streams provide the opportunity for endless building projects, and building dams is addictive, satisfying and frustrating in equal measure.

You can use all sort of materials to build up your dam. Sand is obviously the most effective way to keep water at bay, but is constantly eroded so needs continual maintenance. Stones and wood can add support.

## Remember:

• Many streams will also act as drainage channels following storms and may not be as safe to play in after bad weather. There will usually be signs with warnings to this effect.

# Beach Scavenger Hunt

**Competitive beachcombing – what a great idea! Make sure you look after the environment.**

## You Will Need

A pen and some paper. If some of the finds need to be photographed then the players will need cameras.

## How to Play

A variation on a standard scavenger hunt, this game can be played as individuals or in teams.

First make a list of objects found on a beach that can be collected or photographed. Decide on the points awarded for each item – if some items are trickier to find then they may command a higher number of points. The team that collects the most items on the list within the set time limit wins!

## A Typical List

A feather, a beach ball, a lolly stick, five pieces of litter, three different shells, a stone with a hole through the middle, something red (or another colour), a piece of seaweed, a photo of a sandcastle/fishing boat.

# Boules

**Also known as pétanque, this is a great game to play on a beach. It takes me back to the French Riviera, watching elderly French men and women playing highly competitive games in the warm evening sun.**

## You Will Need

A set of balls – three per player – and a smaller target ball or 'cochonnet'.

## How to Play

Teams can comprise one, two or three players. Toss a coin to choose which team plays first. Any player in this team chooses where to draw a circle on the ground, in which each player will stand to throw their boules.

The same player then throws the cochonnet 4–8m (13–26ft) away from the circle in any direction, at least 1m (3ft) away from any obstacles.

Any player from this team then throws their first boule, trying to get it as close as possible to the cochonnet. When throwing a player's feet must stay together on the ground and inside the circle until the boule has landed.

A player from the opposing team then throws their boule from the circle, trying to get it closer to the cochonnet or knocking their opponent's boule away.

The team with a boule closest to the cochonnet is said to be 'Holding the point'.

The players in the team that is not 'holding' continue to throw until they place a boule closest to the cochonnet, and so on. Players on the same team do not have to take alternate throws, but players must always play their own boules.

When a team has no more boules to be played, the players of the other team throw theirs and try to place them as close as possible to the cochonnet.

## Scoring

When both teams have no more boules, you stop and count up the points. The winning team scores one point for each boule nearer the cochonnet than the opponents' closest. Only one team can score points in each round.

### JOKES WE USED TO TELL

**What is the best day to go to the beach?**
Sunday, of course!

# Ultimate

**Invented in the United States, Ultimate is a team game that uses a disc or Frisbee, with rules loosely based on American Football.**

## You Will Need
A Frisbee or disc.

## How to Play
First determine your playing area. A standard Ultimate field is 37m (40 yards) wide and 110m (120 yards) long; the playing area is 64m (70 yards) long with end zones of 23m (25 yards) at each end, and a standard team has seven players. You can adapt your playing area (and the number of players) to the space available.

The teams decide who will throw first by flipping discs or by 'rock, paper, scissors'. When play begins the team throwing first (the defensive team) must be inside their end zone, and the opposing team (the offensive team) line up on their end zone line. Both teams need to signal their readiness to start by raising a hand, and then play begins with the defensive team throwing the disc to the other team.

Once a player catches or picks up the disc, he or she must stop and keep one foot planted as a pivot until the disc is passed to another player by throwing it (passing the disc hand-to-hand is not allowed). The player has ten seconds to pass the disc and this is counted down by a member of the defensive team, who must remain 3m (10ft) from the player with the disc. This also applies for the offensive team.

If any of the following occur possession transfers to the other team which then becomes the offensive team:

- **the ten-second count expires without the player passing the disc.**
- **the disc is dropped when catching or during the possession.**
- **a pass is blocked, intercepted or not caught.**
- **the disc is thrown out of bounds.**

## Scoring

Goals are scored by a team successfully completing a pass to a player located in the defensive end zone. After a score, the teams switch their direction of attack, and the scoring team throws. Play continues until either team reaches 15 points with a two-point margin over their opponents, or until either team reaches a total of 17 points.

# Beach Memory Game

**Games like this were good when you had finished eating but weren't allowed back in the water until your food had 'gone down'.**

## You Will Need

A stick to draw in the sand, some shells and a towel.

## How to Play

A game for two players. First each player draws a grid in the sand with 16 squares (a four-by-four grid). One player must close their eyes or turn away while the other places shells on certain squares of their grid (only one shell per square) to make a pattern. When it is finished they cover it with a towel.

The other player is now allowed to look at their opponent's grid for five seconds before it is covered up again. Then they try and duplicate the pattern on their own grid. When they have finished they can see how close they got.

For a seaside version of Kim's Game, collect a number of different objects. Let the players look at the objects for a few seconds before covering them up again. The players have to write down as many of the objects as they can remember.

# **Top Ten:** Girls' Names of the 1950s and Now

You only have to watch ten minutes of TV to realise that the most common, traditional names of the 1950s are gradually dying out, making room for a wider variety of names than ever before. A huge difference, but still lots of beautiful girls' names nonetheless!

| 1950 | 2010 |
|---|---|
| 1. Margaret | Olivia |
| 2. Linda | Ruby |
| 3. Mary | Chloe |
| 4. Susan | Emily |
| 5. Deborah | Sophie |
| 6. Barbara | Jessica |
| 7. Joan | Grace |
| 8. Christine | Lily |
| 9. Patricia | Amelia |
| 10. Carol | Evie |

# School Games

No one ever forgets the games they used to play at school, especially the wonderful sounds that those games evoke: marbles clicking in your pocket, the whip of a skipping rope, girls chanting rhymes, the scraping of knees and, of course, the sound of shoes being scuffed beyond repair.

# Jacks

**Dangerously addictive and super-competitive, jacks is just as much fun to play by yourself as it is in a group.**

## You Will Need
Ten metal jacks, one bouncy ball.

## How to Play
The simplest way to play jacks is known as 'Onesies'. Put all the jacks on your playing surface. Throw the ball up in the air and pick up one jack; keep the jack in your hand and catch the ball in the same hand when it has bounced once. Put this jack to one side and then repeat until all the jacks have been collected. If the ball bounces more than once before you pick up a jack then that is a foul.

After you have mastered Onesies you can move on to Twosies – picking up two jacks at a time – and so on, until you are picking up all ten jacks at once.

## Playing in a Group
The first player starts with Onesies and keeps going until he or she fouls. Play then moves to the next player. When the first player gets his or her next turn they start where they left off the last time – if they missed on Threesies then they start on Threesies etc. The first to complete all levels is the winner.

# Clapping Games

**Why is it that you can't remember something that happened last week but you can remember the words to a clapping song you learned when you were five?**

## How to Play

Clapping games are always played with a partner – or two friends if you get very advanced! Begin by clapping your hands together at the same time, then reach out with your right hand to clap your partner's right hand. Next, clap your hands again. Now reach out with your left hand and clap your partner's left hand. Repeat. Always clap on the beat.

The next stage is to start with your left hand up and your right hand down with your partner mirroring you. On the first beat you clap down onto your partner's hands with your left hand and up with the right, on the second beat you clap your partner's hands in front of you, and on the third you clap your hands together. Repeat until the end of the song. This was one of my favourites:

**A sailor went to sea, sea, sea,**
**To see what he could see, see, see,**
**But all that he could see, see, see,**
**Was the bottom of the deep blue sea, sea, sea.**

Miss Mary Mack, Mack, Mack,
All dressed in black, black, black,
With silver buttons, buttons, buttons,
All down her back, back, back.
She asked her mother, mother, mother,
For 50 cents, cents, cents,
To see the elephant, elephant, elephant,
Jump over the fence, fence, fence.
He jumped so high, high, high,
He touched the sky, sky, sky,
And he never came back, back, back,
'Til the fourth of July, ly, ly!

## JOKES WE USED TO TELL

**Knock knock! Who's there?
Isabel! Isabel who?**
Isabel necessary on a bike?

# French Skipping

**The cause of quite a few grazed knees as I recall. This was the game that everyone wanted to be the best at.**

## You Will Need
A length of elastic around 5mm (¼in) wide, and three players – or one player and two chairs if you're desperate!

## How to Play
Two players stand facing each other with the elastic stretched quite tight around their ankles to form a long rectangle and the third player has to perform a series of jumps and hops, singing a rhyme at the same time. For example:

**Peanut cookies, when you bake,**
**How many minutes will you take?**
**One, two, three, four, five.**

On 'one' the player has to jump up and land facing sideways with the right foot in the middle of the loop and the left foot outside.

On 'two' they have to jump and land with the left foot in the middle and the right foot outside.

On 'three' they have to jump and land with both feet outside the elastic.

On 'four' they have to jump and land with both feet on top of the elastic.

On 'five' it gets really hard as they have to jump and land with both feet outside the elastic then shuffle round to face the other way, so the elastic makes a zig-zag shape around their legs, then jump out and land with their feet on top of the elastic.

If they manage this tricky task, the elastic is raised to knee height for another round, then thigh height and finally waist height for French Skipping superstars. When they get it wrong, it's the next person's turn, and the first person has to start from scratch again next time.

Another popular chant was this one:

**England, Ireland, Scotland, Wales,**
**Inside, outside, inside, on!**

# Skipping

**One of my favourite school games that we just never seemed to get tired of. Although it was mostly the girls that played, you could guarantee that when the boys joined in they would try to show us who was best!**

## You Will Need

A regular rope for skipping by yourself or with a partner, a longer (7.5m/25ft) rope for playing in a larger group – and a loud voice for chanting.

## Partner Games

These just use a regular skipping rope and usually one other person. The one I remember most is this one.

### 'I Like Coffee, I Like Tea'

Start off skipping on your own. As you skip, say the following rhyme, including your friend's name:

**'I like coffee, I like tea, I like Julie in with me!'**

Now your friend jumps in and skips with you and you say:

**'I don't like coffee, I don't like tea. I don't like Julie in with me!'**

Your friend must now jump out of your skipping rope as you skip. Keep going for as long as you can without stopping.

## Group Games

For these games you need the longer rope and two people to turn it ('enders'). Our favourites included:

**Bumper Car, Bumper Car**
For this game you take turns to jump in and say:
**Bumper car, bumper car number 48,**
**Went around the corner** (at which point you run out, around one of the enders and back in the other side),
**And slammed on the brakes** (here you stop the rope between your legs).

**Teddy Bear, Teddy Bear**
One at a time, jump in and skip to this rhyme and do the actions described as you say it:

**Teddy bear, teddy bear, turn around,**
**Teddy bear, teddy bear, touch the ground,**
**Teddy bear, teddy bear, go upstairs,**
**Teddy bear, teddy bear, say your prayers,**
**Teddy bear, teddy bear, switch off the light,**
**Teddy bear, teddy bear, say goodnight.**

If you stop the rope or miss any of the actions you are out. When out, swap with one of the people turning the rope.

# What's the Time, Mr Wolf?

**Full of suspense, and quite scary when you are young, this game always makes a lot of noise.**

## How to Play

One player is chosen to be Mr Wolf. Mr Wolf stands at the opposite end of the playing area from the other players, facing away from them. The group calls out: 'What's the time, Mr Wolf?' He replies with a time, for example, 'It's two o'clock.'

The group then takes two steps forward and asks again, 'What's the time, Mr Wolf?' This time he might say, 'It's ten o'clock,' in which case the group would take ten steps forwards.

Their aim is to reach Mr Wolf without him first catching them. When Mr Wolf senses someone is close, instead of calling a time, he can shout 'It's dinner time!' and can finally turn around and see where everybody is, and then try to catch someone before they can make it back to the starting line.

### Tip

Taking big steps means you are in with a chance of catching the wolf but also means you are in the firing line when it's dinner time!

# Grandmother's Footsteps

**I always tried to make sure I was standing on two legs at all times – otherwise I would be sure to wobble.**

## How to Play

Choose one person to be Grandmother. She (or he) stands at one end of the playing area while the other players stand on a line (real or imaginary) about 10m (33ft) away. While Grandmother's back is turned the players try to sneak up on her but whenever she turns around the players have to freeze. Anyone who is caught moving must go back to the start. The first person to touch Grandmother takes over for the next round.

## NAME-CALLING

You may also know this game as: 'Red Light, Green Light', 'Statues' or 'Sly Fox'.

---

### JOKES WE USED TO TELL
**What's black and white and red all over?**
A newspaper!

---

# Mother, May I?

**Another one of my favourites – if your friend was 'Mother' you knew you had a good chance of winning!**

## How to Play

For three or more players. Choose one person to be 'Mother' (can be 'Captain' or 'Father' if boys don't want to be 'Mother'!). The rest of the group stands in a line facing them a fair distance away. Your aim is to reach Mother but you must take it in turns and can only move according to her instructions.

Mother gives instructions to each player in turn, for example, 'Olivia, take one giant and three baby steps'. Olivia must say, 'Mother, may I?' and then take her steps. If you forget to say 'Mother, may I?' or get the step wrong you must return to the start. The first player to reach Mother is the winner.

## Different Types of Steps

Baby steps (steps the exact length of your foot); regular steps; giant steps (the biggest steps you can make); bird steps (tiny steps with toes pointed out putting your heel halfway along the inside of the opposite foot for each step); bunny/frog steps (hops); banana step (where you lie down with your feet at their current spot, noting where the top of your head is, and standing up there for your new position).

# Duck, Duck, Goose

**Popular all over the world, this game definitely gets you warmed up on a cold day.**

## How to Play

For five or more players. The players sit in a large circle facing inwards. One player is chosen to be 'It' and walks around the outside of the circle. As 'it' walks around, he or she touches each child gently on the head saying, 'Duck, Duck, Duck.'

At some point 'it' will say, 'Goose' instead of 'Duck'. The 'Goose' must then jump up and chase 'it' around the circle. 'It' must then try to get all the way back to the Goose's place without getting caught.

If 'it' gets there safely, the Goose becomes it and the game starts again. If the Goose catches 'it', the same person must try to catch the next Goose.

## NAME-CALLING

You may also know this game as: 'The Mush Pot', 'Duck, Duck, Grey Duck', 'Rag Tag', or 'Drop the Handkerchief'.

# Paper, Scissors, Stone

**Invented in the Far East, this classic playground duel demands quick hands and quick thinking.**

## How to Play

This hand game is for two players, often played as a 'best of three' match. Together the players hold out one hand in a fist and count 'One, two, three' before making one of the three signs below at the same time:

- **Paper: an open hand.**
- **Scissors: index and middle fingers used to imitate scissors.**
- **Stone: a clenched fist.**

The outcomes are as follows:

- **Stone blunts scissors: stone defeats scissors.**
- **Scissors cut paper: scissors defeats paper.**
- **Paper covers stone: paper defeats stone.**

If the players make the same sign, that that round is not counted. We tried to play as fast as we could – the problem with that was we always lost count of who was winning!

# **Top Ten:** Boys' Names of the 1950s and Now

Even though many of the most popular boys' names have remained the same over the years, try and recall when you last heard a boy being called his actual name? Boys much prefer calling each other nicknames. So, instead of James, Oliver, Thomas and William you get Jimmy, Olly, Tommy and Billy instead!

| 1950 | 2010 |
|---|---|
| 1. James | Oliver (Olly) |
| 2. Robert | Jack (Jacky) |
| 3. John | Harry ('Arry) |
| 4. Michael | Alfie (Alf) |
| 5. David | Joshua (Josh) |
| 6. William | Thomas (Tommy) |
| 7. Richard | Charles (Charlie) |
| 8. Thomas | William (Billy) |
| 9. Charles | James (Jimmy) |
| 10. Stephen | Daniel (Danny) |

# Chalk Games

Whether I was at home or at school, if I had a piece of chalk and a concrete surface I was happy. The boys may not have liked Hopscotch as much as the girls, but they were more than happy to hijack our chalk so they could play Tic-tac-toe or Hangman.

# Marbles

**Who didn't love marbles – smooth, shiny and glittering like playground jewels. In our games we strived desperately to keep hold of all of our own marbles while winning the prized possessions of our friends.**

## You Will Need

Each player will need one large shooter marble (2cm/¾in) and a selection of regular (1.5cm/⅝in) marbles. Chalk for drawing lines.

## How to Play

For two or more players. Draw two circles on the ground: the inner circle should be about 30cm (1ft) in diameter and the outer circle about 2m (7ft). Players must agree on the number of marbles to be placed in the inner circle, and then they take turns to shoot their larger marble from any point on the outer ring at the marbles in the centre.

If the shooter manages to knock any of the marbles out of the inner ring he or she is entitled to keep them and also to shoot again from where the shooter marble has landed.

If the shot is unsuccessful the shooter marble stays where it is (if it is inside the outer ring) and play passes to the next player who may shoot at the marbles inside the inner ring or at any of the other shooter marbles. If a player strikes a shooter marble, the owner of that marble must give the shooter one of his or her marbles to get it back, and the shooter takes another shot. Play continues until the ring is cleared.

## And the Winner is ...

The person with the most marbles at the end of the game. But are you playing 'Keepsies' or 'Fairsies'? The former means the winners get to keep all the marbles they have won, while the latter means that all marbles are returned to their rightful owners at the end of the game – make sure you agree on this before you start the game!

**Tip**

Throwing, flicking and rolling are all techniques you can use to launch your marble. Shooting your marble 'knuckle down' – placing the knuckle of your index finger on the ground with your finger curling up, sitting the marble in the crook of your finger and then using your thumb to flick the marble towards its target – is a good way to get a lot of force behind your shot.

# Hopscotch

When I was at school this game got so competitive we tried to find the most accurate marker we could. Stones would bounce and beanbags were usually locked away so we settled on short lengths of necklace chain. Believe me, it worked!

## You Will Need

Chalk for drawing the grid, a stone or beanbag to be a marker.

# How to Play

For two or more players. First mark out your grid. These do vary but the one shown here seems to be the most common.

Decide the order of play. The first player throws his or her marker into square number 1. They must then move along the grid hopping on one foot on single squares and planting two feet on double squares.

When they reach number 10 they turn around and come back using the same technique. When they reach their marker they pick it up and return to the start.

# Remember:

· **The beanbag must land within the square. If it lands outside the grid, on a different square or on the line of the square, it is considered a misthrow and you miss your go.**

· **When you are moving through the grid you must not land on the lines or outside the grid. If you do either of these you must return to the start and wait for your next go.**

· **If you put your other foot down when you are supposed to be on one leg you must return to the start.**

· **You mustn't put your foot in the square where your marker is.**

# Tic-tac-toe

This doesn't have to be played using chalk but paper tends to blow around outside so it makes things easier on a windy day.

## You Will Need

Chalk – one piece for each player is probably best.

## How to Play

This is a game for two players. First draw a simple four-line grid creating nine spaces (three rows of three). One player is 'X' and the other '0'. Traditionally the person who is 'X' goes first but that is up to you!

The first player places his or her mark in one space in the grid, then the second player does the same. The aim of the game is to get three of your marks in a row either horizontally, vertically or diagonally. The player that succeeds in doing this is the winner.

## NAME-CALLING

You may also know this game as: 'Noughts and Crosses, 'Xs and Os' or 'Three-in-a-row'.

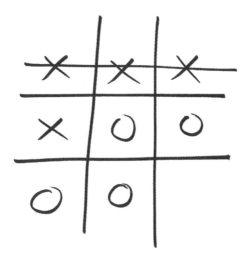

# Hangman

**This was a real favourite of mine. I can still remember racking my brains to try and guess the word before my opponent drew the last leg of the hanging man.**

## You Will Need
One piece of chalk.

## How to Play
This is usually a game for two players but the person guessing may well need some extra help!

The first player thinks of a word and draws a row of dashes to represent each letter of the word. The second player then needs to guess the letters in the words. If he or she suggests a letter that does occur in the word, the other player writes it in where it appears (this may be more than once). If the suggested letter does not appear the first player draws one element of the hangman diagram.

## The Diagram
Once again these vary depending on where you learned to play this game. The version I know contained 12 elements, as seen here. This means you can suggest up to 11 incorrect letters before you lose the game.

The game is over when the word is completed or guessed correctly or the first player completes the hangman diagram.

## Tip:

* Choose vowels and other common letters first (R, T, N, S, L, C) – there is more chance of these letters appearing in the word and a greater chance that you will guess it.

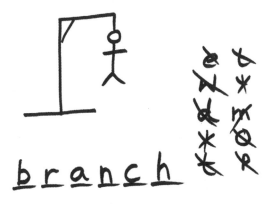

branch